11368

"If you change the way you look at things,
the things you look at change"
- Dr. Wayne Dyer

by

Roseann Geiger

CONTENTS

DEDICATION

"To my left leg, without whom I would wobble, because life is most beautiful when you dance"

ISBN: 978-81-8253-964-8

First Edition: 2022
Rs. 200/-

Cyberwit.net
HIG 45 Kaushambi Kunj, Kalindipuram
Allahabad - 211011 (U.P.) India
http://www.cyberwit.net
Tel: +(91) 9415091004
E-mail: info@cyberwit.net

Printed at VCORRE PRESS.

& Whimsey

I'd like to wade
in a whiskey bottle
Rum rushing through
ten thirsty toes
A splash of soda
to cool my shoulders
An apple red cherry
to garnish my nose.
I'd love to fly
along a lullaby
Meet a mockingbird
over the moon
Share a star's teeny twinkle
fetch stray babes in a bough
Let black sheep
keep his chic swirly wool.

11368

You lost so much
Your losses are mine
welcoming woods
I lay buried within your wilds
in the heart of you
beside butterflies and bees
at Paul's pulpit
appropriately, with the memory
of rest between worlds
and child wonder quizzing
A bridge so near
and there, another
seeks dinosaurs
beyond big footed gods
and the world where I lay
at a point in time, all
was about the infinite
and naive to harm
This version of me rides empty
a tether sharing the pain
Your pain
echoing along the paths
that Amodeo laid
before he swiped his benches
Your pain is mine
and I will rise on a day
like the column
Not so old, or perhaps older
I wouldn't know
I will rise when you
fed up with the world
abandon your crown

and open earth to swallow
misdeed, and memory will jut
from your man-made waters
memory of life lived in your wilds
mushroom hunters and exhibitionists
all dreaming of futures
and loving your ground
I wait to rise with you
like a bride
be born again, my past, my soul
Teach me the future
I am hungry for it
because the now is gray.

A Loan in High Heels

If you could picture perfect
you would see a little boy
crowned in golden curls
with flickering blue eyes
and a smile...a smile...
he'd be beyond precocious
a toddler toddling in your high heels
who, if that weren't funny enough
would grab two gallons of olive oil
and proceed on his stroll
he'd make you want your own child
and when you were pregnant
he'd help you practice
sleep in bed with you
laugh and whack you in the face
when the sun rose
he'd pick off your plate
cucumbers and pickles being his favorite
all kinds of busy
this kid would make you tired
and he would grow
more alchemic than real
he'd be brilliant
an athlete, a musician, an artist
a doctor, if he chose
and when the other kids were scattering
he would entertain
he'd laugh with you, dance with you
twirl little ones in the air
he'd pop up when you didn't expect him
and drop everything if you called.
I assume every family has one

some more famous than others
Alex the Great
Ed the Black Prince
JFK the Junior
taken too soon or sooner
than we're ready for
this golden child would always be a loan
we mythicize the ancient gods
but they still play their tricks
the gifted are bought and paid for
we have no rights, no claims
we show them off
we call them ours
they break dance
and we dream for them
but when the old gods cash in
their dance is done
alchemy sets in reverse,
alone in high heels
we slip and tumble on tears.

A Snowflake

and you are no more hero
than assassin
hiding and waiting
for me to throw
my body raw
into a volcano
Passion dies like
fresh snow
sad and dirty
in a lattice of soot
smothering brief beauty
your gift to me
a snowflake
incomparable
and dying
gone before I can
hold it in my hand
like another birthday
your footprint
would be stamped
on my heart
if only I had one
left to trod.

The Alarm Clock

He spews orders like dogma
at varying intervals
"Ding-a-ling!"
Time to tell her what to do.
She responds
in her child-voice
forever branded
the rebel adolescent
spitting shock values
begging, begging
for five minutes more.

Artifice

Eyes bite into seconds
meeting pleas with pretense,
kindlings cunningly embellished
in skillfully masked menace splice,
one thing leads
and another follows lamely,
without revelation or fiber,
there are no questions raised
when monsters are bred
just carefully enough.

Asylum

Somehow
I never nightmare.
Philosophies drone
into my brain
Experts enlist in
pseudo-surgery with
spoons and straws
extracting logic
injecting bedlam
salvation, stirred, shaken, scrambled.
Meanwhile,
mock falcons plunge
and clutch my eyes
replacing reality
with memory
I watch the same scenes
again, again.
It always starts with a kiss
then slurs.

At a Point

I am in my red now
my tresses change color
soon they will wither
and perhaps fall
perhaps I will become the tree
my bark lined with stories
dreams furrowed
alongside my blight
into destinies, still forming
and transforming
into the rustling crescent
ever changing and beholding
secrets in silent boughs
and nests of starts
that molt and tumble
when long quit,
but attrition is life,
new genesis embarks
within wrinkly dactyls
until, on the last day
I am delivered, slain and shorn
I am as always mere kindling
for those who would root
in my ember, in my war.

At Dusk

Waning concepts
fly suddenly
from twilight toward
unknown peaks
of purple orange
reality boots up.
The mirror does its job
and reflects
on naughts
and splurgings
kicking aside productivity
nudging unbridled hysterias
reaching to undo time.

Awareness

I almost left it behind
but that voice
like a finger snap
dimples my logic
and I return from
fossil state,
calibrating.
Without tears
or anxiety anymore
I slip in under the radar
coerced into re-musing
I arrive, again, without a plan.
Here I go
fresh paint over rust
It doesn't take long
to stain, again
but it does get easier
to slip back out
before I'm realized,
even by myself.

Bipolar

Lady
Two Faces

You were never two faced.
One came first
and then the other.
Your soul is their mangled battleground.

Your heart could spin
beats into gold.
Your monster can rip
meat from bones.

People love you in limbo
like cinema behind bars.
They watch you wage war
while each face kills the other.

Lady Two Faces
mind crumbling in tow.

Bricks

Sometimes im slow to think
But if promises were bricks...
I guess I should start at the beginning
On the first day, God created light
It was definitely good
But we've never learned
to navigate the shadows
Is a promise a word given
to guarantee a commitment
if so, it's just a lie, right?
Nothing can be guaranteed
and there's the beauty of it
broken contracts
lawyers make millions over their consequence
broken hearts conjure all sorts of art
articulating the beauty of the broken
music conveys brotherhood
a collateral family, robbed
of the myth, of the promise
then there's the unspoken promise
is there anything more intangible?
And when they break
in their imperceptible way
Is there anything more painful?
Shakespearean slings and arrows
invisible, yet powerful,
the phrase, "I promise"
to whoever, to do whatever
so powerful that legions run off
thirsting for a shadow
a promise sparks fire
vernacular phosphorus

what makes that any different
than a birthday cake wish?
People heap promises in quantum
bricklaying into one big Schrodingic con
The lives we lay so exquisitely
vanish when we open the door
You see, on the first day, God created light
It was definitely good
But we've never learned
to navigate the shadows.

Centrifuge

Eventually
in a world unworthy of
its averageness
words play forward
and unprotected
from candor's menace
daring to dream
where Shakespeare stumbles
and opinions end.
Eventually
shades of grey give way
into a maelstrom
and channel
pure white
and black
so deliberate that
tact is eclipsed
ambiguity expunged.
Air brushed skin is pierced
and spilling blood
crimson and laden
with tonic
and prejudice.

Cha Cha

He scries, scowling, into his oracle
The sports page
deciphering cryptics concealed
within news print; He prophesies:
Cowboys by seven;
Teabisquit by a nose...
He gathers his tribe of keys,
kisses his spouse
a pink cheeked Earth Mother,
her white tresses tousling in his wake,
and departs, grumbling,
on his daily war path,
battling store clerks
bellowing cusses at motorists,
returning, arms laden
with food and trinkets
for fortunate kinfolk
returning to a petite Pocahantas
Little bare feet slaps announce
a head-dress of golden ringlets
She pushes them aside
with a tiny hand
that pulls her great Chief
Cha Cha
Into her play tent
to pow wow.

Chelsea

Cherubs blow candied kisses at
Her as she sings her silly songs
Evoking
Laughter from sadly serious hearts and
Sunbeams from her painted toes
Every star winks a wish
At the prettiest eyes, pink lips and smoochable nose.

Clockweed

A record of circumstance
a recipe for psychiatric suicide
a nameless purpose, curls
within arbitrary seeking
lurks slightly above natural law
courting assault from falsehoods
that exist partially and in synergy
with wrong turns and dead-ended promises.
Time powers hope less long than ardent
trusting logic to heal fear.
A rushed tribute ends
without the expected cry
of anger at onslaught.
You should have stayed the long and known
you could have pulled a honeybee
by its tail, kissed nectar from its feet
and enjoyed a spray of spoils
instead of yielding to self-starvation
instead of ducking the blow.
You allow it to be what it chooses.

Communicable

He lauds every self-spoken word
in silent pompous beaming
back-patting predacious humor
and spewing himself
over any sorry contact.

Some speak to communicate
Some to spread their disease.

.Converted

Gospels lick at urchins
who lazily respond
Some things look very pretty
but make no sense at all.
A mind like a buttercup
blossoming turbulence
preys on vestiges
of puerile opulence.
A feral peach
rebirths carnal sucklings
who coo affectionately
to discordant lullabies.
It all appears normal
preachers harvest their ripest
and steep them like fine teas
Zealous in their industry
they endure
turning foundlings on a spit
to convince and connive
sweet lambkins parlay savagery
beautiful things hide their souls

deliberation

stockings not hung lay prone
below a week's worth of trappings
still boastIng red
reminding me, too busy
to speak of patience,
to yield and muster
seasons overwhelm
but puppies still snuggle
children still yearn
and life lives but only an instant

Devoid

I unearth you
each layer a major find
but much work
for an empty hand
What light do I hope for?
Ma che importa?
all I hold are a voice and a promise
Whether you are a memory
or a fantasy
you're not tangible
even a shadow
is a better companion.

Dialogue

They are a duo I just can't figure
same time, each morning, she
sits and waits with her book
or her knitting
maybe it's crochet
she's always dressed casually
she always faces his way
and he, obviously the alpha
old coot, stands at the track
book in hand, impeccably dressed
always in the same spot
facing the track, anticipating
They arrive together every morning
and wait at their spots
some distance from each other
not speaking, never touching
not even in bad weather
when sometimes they wait inside.
As the train arrives, he straightens
she slowly approaches his flank
and enters at his heal
they sit together silently
she seems to know the rules
and reads or knits
he reads the paper, then his book.
I wouldn't know they existed
had he not admonished me, once
on that first train ride, when she too spoke
her head popping about as she
barked about my rudeness
although it wasn't the "quiet car"
I obviously wasn't aware of their rules,

but I became aware of them
arriving, departing, not speaking
for years I assumed by their looks.
perplexed, I'd ponder
where do they go?
what ARE they to each other?
standing, sitting, walking, together
every day, never touching.
They argued once, sort of
he scolded her, "Give it up",
and "What?", she asked
he countered, "Give it up, I said"
and she stomped away
to the other end of the track.
Sometimes when I see them
hurrying out toward their car
I want to follow them
I want to see where they live,
these people who don't smile
or touch or speak
I wonder what she had to "give up"
as she bolts ahead in the parking lot
like a befuddled hound unleashed.

Evanescence

Roses may table their own death.
At their most striking
they are a dying thing
one delicate frame lodges
past, present and what's to be.
Stems and thorns clipped into the sink
they pose red, tender and temporary
Minutes of fame vibrate
above the lip of an urn
Flame and fade.
All things decay
except the menace of tomorrow.

Familial Felicity

When they die
we turn to counterfeit happiness
paper lanterns with painted faces
a desperate emulation of past perfect.
Bulimic memory
the closest thing to laughter
Search and upchuck
Search and upchuck.

flirt like Dali

mother sleeps beneath
a sweating peach
avoiding the crush of logic
far away in another language
a symphony melts down
into meat and music
no one can hear the moan
of fish ripping
against tide and slamming
into a rusted bow
partially because squid
boast so loudly
mainly because
the ocean buries sound
mother curses her skin
pale and crinkling
while she juices the wind
for coins and voices
the vastness of expense
drains muscle
puckers lips against
the drum of tree bark
and whips the sun itself
into a shadow.

Grave Walkers

Memories darken
then surface
only through
a silvered stream
caught against night
It surges and charms
a somniloquy
from abandoned lips
Crusting eyes
throw remnants,
a cairn
to mark the spot
where figments lie.
Lies color and scent
like flowers
stars and butterflies
each one, a mortal image
and no more than an
illusion dressed in thorns
stinging and burning.
After beauty fades
after scent dispels
into air and earth
and after flutters
abandon skin tingling
in consequence of
bygone strumming
we are left
with only questions
of their existence.

If Only...

If this were 1980
I would pass you a note
while we sat not listening
to a strange professor more interested in whatever
lurked beyond classroom windows
than he was in us anyway.
If we met before the damage
when I was red, ripe and shiny
with my new girl smell
I would courtly love the crap out of you
with notes, not desires
and we would walk halls like those other kids
hands touching and bodies close
planning all the things we would do alone
If that was 1980 and love wasn't secret now
would we escape ourselves long enough to fill each other
would we block out the world
and pass love notes
If we did in 1980?

Impostulating

I would have bought the shirt
what a foolish woman I have become
to assume that I can buy happy
I'm no better with my person
when I stop giving myself
who am I?
And why do I give me all away?
I oscillate
I confiscate
I perpetuate
the lie of me
yes sir
no sir
can do, will do
doing, doing
on faith alone
am I a true believer?
or a kitemaster
moving always,
hoofing in ponzi pumps?

in session

winter whistles, slow
and silky white.
it sprays corners
midnight heavy
stage setting
for a new span
of idle indoor chortle.
society re-acquaints
with its vernacular
containing bustle
and slobbering etiquettes
on hardwood floors.
Compressed, inside days
Mornings plumped
Like frozen water.
The out of bed experience
Cracks drowsy spines
Like a frigid whip.
Doors open
Cumulus fangs
Hurl icy venom
Eyes tear
Teeth clack
Snakebite on the rocks.

Inferno

Who could discern
the deep darkness
of your soul?

Your eyes, a kiln of hell-fire
so torrid so alluring,
a serpent's stare holding me frozen
in all but my desire.

Candied apples in your eyes,
luscious spellbinding persuasions,
seduce me with fool's gold
and shapeless promises.

I teeter on a slippery line,
cool security pleading,
serpentine eyes beckoning...

"Come on in,
the fire's fine".

Interlude

the day is midnight
sexy black
I feel your breath
in winds that tap
tap my shoulders
run through my hair and
down my hip
and under there
if you were a raindrop
trailing my breast
I could trap you
for a moment
moist hot and suddenly cool
like a breeze after cloudbursts
your wetness tattooed
and your memory
tingling full yet gone

The Jellyfish

Your eyes still knock on my back door
Keeping time with my pulse.
Your eyes,
Myopic enigma
Haunting me,
Holding me taut
For the elusive warmth of your smile.
Your eyes,
Drawing, reeling me in,
I remain helpless,
Eager, to writhe
At the end of their line -
My compulsive jellyfish rapture.

Leonid's Little Boat

Frail wave
violet water
layers yielding shadow

life is frail
the water whistles siren song

little boat
you sail on blue orange violet
the waters run parallel
the other ocean tells a different story
the layers yield a shadow

life is fragile
bubbles hold cures and curses

little boat on violet waves
you speak a maelstrom
your beauty pulls my eye
its colors are rapture
but your sea sings the din

life lies its frail lies within.

let it be

you need at least a hair out of place
one crinkle in your pants
one line on your face
you need a chip or a dent
here or there
a scratch where you tickle
and freckles somewhere
life breeds scrapes and wrinkles
we get clobbered by love
the most fulfilling existence
is one worn like a glove.

Lewd Thoughts

I sit here thinking of stained glass
while you peruse your black and white.
All of the things that I can't do
taunt me as you roll up your sleeves.
How dare you stoke my greedy imagination
by being here
Mister,
Put those arms away!

Life after death

Waxing sad
I dare to open thought
accepting your demise
but you are no dead thing
you breathe, you work
play and live
yanking life only from me
I mourn now
tired of yearning
and older than the corpse
you brought to life
by whim.
Waxing now
into exile, I mourn
and feign a heart
without break
but a heart.
It will shard and scatter
when you exhale
your wordless “good-bye”
I will cease
and be a new form of scarred
but first I will mourn
for wonder
for desire

for tears
I mourn my libido
that longing, yearning thing
that flaps its wings inwardly
beating drums, strumming strings
I mourn all of the thoughts
strung into days
a wreath of you
like a holiday from fear
that will remain, unmourned
and undead
no trick of you
is strong enough
to rid what waits
silent with fingertips
and soft kisses
to terrorize this life
so I mourn most of all
something beautiful
something infamous
a metaphor of ignorance.

Loiterer

Your image,
a malfunctioning promise
idles in my handbag.
I took that picture
when I took your word
never expecting both to be
two dimensional.
I can't breathe life into your promises
any more than I can infuse it
into your photograph
but at least I have something tangible
in your picture.
Your promise remains a myth.

Messenger

is there time
to ask a question
when the order
is transmitted from
creator to cohort?
whose proponent
drains the color
from your cheek
and sends a myriad
of winged gestation
to accompany
your segue
from one life to
an alleged other?

Mistletoe

You got your wings
too soon I know
every time I see
that mistletoe
Corny days and frosty haze
when we were young
we laughed without end
But life gave us different stories
yours was short and sweet
my friend
My memories fade
yet here I am longing
to see u someday
under that mistletoe
I walk winter windows
Gift wishes, tie bows
Living's good
This time of year
But each time I see
that kissing tree
my heart recalls joy
and sheds tears
Still, I don't look for signs
to know your still mine
I just send you
my bittersweet cheer
under that mistletoe
each year

Mobius Strip

irises washed with night
swirling spheres
tapering into
purple powdered pirouettes
then a road
there is always more
tomorrow is pulled under a carpet
blue faced and dream drunk
enough to create another dawn
and a breath, just enough
to arise, crusty and smelling
like rump
then a road, and a twist
a cleansing and sowing
a blossom of iris
there is always more...

My Monster

I could easily hate you
for making me wait
for tapping this feeling
buried long and deep
for panicking me
with what you desire
then making me wait
and long for tiny seeds
whispered within my ear
to plant and grow
into the very thing
that I fear the most.
My guarded replies
come from lips too ripe
to protest, yet burdened
with fear so intense
and too intense to conjure
unlocking words.
My arousal
trapped and building
presses me hard
and in secret
I could easily hate you
for that, for your way of
seducing me toward
some unknown and
unwanted disaster, for
making me ache for
more of your mischief
and making me long
to be taunted in ways
I never expected.
But I don't feel anything

near to hate as
I feel the hum of
your words inside
rooting and tangling
in that spot, marked
for a grave, yanking
buried feeling, making it
burn and open into
a clumsy beast
yearning and terrified.

<u>My Morning Wrap</u>

slow walkers
close talkers
too early stalkers
my morning wrap,
seat hoggers
stair stoppers
gotta be a bag hopper
my morning wrap,
bad news
winter blues
screw these soggy shoes
my morning wrap,
eyes blinkin
boulevard stinkin
what am I thinkin?
My morning wrap,
predators prowling
buses growling
my stomach is howling,
my morning wrap,
bills left in my kitchen
bloodsuckers bitchin
my pockets are itchin
my morning wrap
chains grow around me
life don't come cheaply
cant get away freely
my morning wrap.

Nephilim

I assume that we are carved
from native bits of fleshy earth
until we resemble beings
that can withstand baths steeped
severely in malice and idiocy
without losing that breath
entrusted within us
the breath that gives voice,
objecting voice, at the wars
word ones or otherwise
that rob us of simple dignities.
I assume that, but
there must be a slope
where some slip
that rips and pokes,
scrambles the messages
that we are meant to share.
Okay, the angels were imperfect but
some beings live like lumpy earth
greatly squandered and ill used.

<u>Ode to those who know nothing</u>

Our world is bound in laws
binding writs that encompass
life, death and protection
of those and all matters between.
Carefully crafted by accidental authors
our rules serve a purpose
of employing lawmakers
Those who dictate need not know,
those who speak need only to speak
their words need not be correct or true.
The rare overlord words thoughts
born of mind and channeled
toward a lust for righteousness
Frankly, rarity may be imagined
and wisdom a fantasy
We gather round naked emperors
eager for any falsehood
to validate fit and whim.

On a Dig

while clearing cobwebs
from my mind, and other places,
I came across your things
I forgot what I kept
old driver's licenses
that ring with the chip…
I could have had the white gold
with the diamond and sapphire
but I chose the black
since it was your favorite.
I'm sure you were wearing it
when you fell, but the chip was
there, already, and
I remember that you wanted to
get it fixed, I was with you, of course
and the jeweler just shook his head
the onyx would only split,
but it was your favorite,
that's how it goes.
I would have kept you
in any condition
I never prayed for you to die
even if that's what you wanted.
I wanted you fixed
I wanted you to still be
your doctors just shook their heads
but you were my favorite
and that's how it goes.

Ouroboros Darkly

to whine, or not
to whine or wine
we the extraordinary ordinary
career ourselves
picking bones, unforensically
and seeking universal truths
in a vacuum
the alchemical power of complaint
transforms us, uncathartically
and we the self sanctified
settle into our prickly nests
not surprisingly bewildered
so we repeat,
discerning faults, sharpening tongues
raising the pitch of our cries
deftly refining until we hear
our mewling voice alone
and when we wake
once again
choking on our tails
we the feckless stumble
into a new day, wondering
just wondering
and always wondering
why?

Pain

Surprising extravagance
for some, the envied spike of a realness
that the bored and the boring
would gladly trade for their mundane.
The afflicted pray for a pass on the cup
for new life, for a life, any life
especially one strewn with boredom
as seeking in circles would be paradise.
We arrive within senses
feel, wonder, and look about
then we want what isn't close
Seeing hearing touching being
aren't enough when what's out beckons

pase lo que pase

Flicking off protocol
I tie my pen
to a postage stamp
its image pierced
by inky fallout
and tempered with an arc
of sticky colored gas
It catches chatter
and quarrelsome greetings
on its way
in and out
of a mail bag
Gathering gossipy yakety-yak
it grows fat filling
on bogus prattle
until its delivery
onto an old lap
like crude gospel
on a Sunday afternoon.

Penn Station

alone, they sit,
each one, alone
freckling the room
like beads of sweat
they spring from chairs
and floor,
wordlessly waiting
to be swept aside
by billy club or broom,
only to reappear
like immortal tears
of fallen angels.

Pocket of Thorns

Your words linger longer than they should
maybe I should have a sense stronger to stay away

You say we need to be more than living,
but abandoned armor is certain suicide
I've made it this far by blocking my hurting
so I fill my pockets with your whispers
until I'm somewhere safe enough to feel

and your words linger longer than they should
maybe I should have a sense stronger to stay away

I string your words between my fingers
I read them over and over until I blur,
until my mind leaves my body open
until your voice, in tiny flames,
licks the salt from my living wounds

and your words linger longer than they should
maybe I should have a sense stronger to stay away

Your whispers spin roses in my pockets
I reach for them until I bleed, like a fool,
forgetting to respect the thorn
but I don't care because bleeding makes me feel
I don't care because blood and thorns are real

and your words linger longer than they should
maybe I should have a sense stronger to stay away.

Polarity

I had no money
to fund your special day
so I took out my heart
and wrapped it in a box,
Sealed with kisses
Filled with wishes
Magic, Moonbeams
Meaningful stuff.

You aspired more materially
I instantly surmised
As I watched you rip open the wrapping
Shake up and down
Then toss my gift aside
Not only missing the point
But looking, amidst your disbelief
For more.

Since I should have known better
I stoically accepted
your face-slapping gratitude
Since I should have known better
I watched you plod my heart parts
and since I knew better
I crouched and gathered
me, broken, and discarded myself
once more.

Polish

Painted pink and pretty
they lie like smiles
like my spirit
manicured by a mushroom
Chips and scratches neatly hidden
by a psychedelic stigma
flake off gradually
in shards of congealed alchemy.
I am not alone in magical dissembling
We walk a grave here and there
and improve on life, on the ravages
we color, we paint pretty
on tumors and wars.
Layers lacquer the dying within
and we live dissembled
cloaked in matte
or pearl, or glitter
polished until pulled
by the tomb tailing our feet.

Prospector

I wonder often
what do you do with them,
the many jewels mined
from my rankled mind.

Jagged edged gems scraping,
my brain further chafing
as you unearth each disturbing bauble.

I wonder often
if your excavation
reveals some personal fruit
or some prized, torture bred treasure.

What do you do
with your collection of stone and marl?
Do you display your torment born trinkets?

Do they sit in your studio, up high
on a laminated shelf and buffed
to painstaking perfection,
reflecting the light of your merciless labor

Herr lover's pride and joy?

Reckoning

The piper is born
with his own coin to spend
each year, a barter,
fun for premium.
Every vice has a price,
like to smoke?
20 years you say?
That'll cost you 20
cocaine? Another 20
needle? 35
You got game?
Sex unbridled?
Let's spin the wheel
uh oh
today is not your lucky day,
a year or two and you're away.

Reeds

Men break things
Women especially
They take them apart
One piece at a time
Until they can't function
No matter,
Women are smarter
If they repair
After a break
They learn to bend

Shadows of Doubt

It's much colder
than it appears to be
in the shimmering
behind the mist
of the washing surf,
It holds wet breath
pulling back
then releasing a slap
to rouse a sleeping beach.
Luminaries count
hours with waves
like proverbial sheep
pirated by a yawn
until sunrise.
Beyond the crossed needs
of night and day
a draught of stars
tingles against dampness
lingering like frost
on curves of strand.
This echo of play sings
into first light as
we endure the shadow side
seeking the difference
between delusion
and the working self.
I remain still
yet well awake
within your embrace
uninformed, as usual
and dismayed
trying to hide
inside unraveling vows

clinging, as equilibrium melts
and I crash into waves
assaulted, again and again.

Sine Qua Non(without which, not)

To lie flat
and face my skies
my history flooding back
filling moment with memory
more so, making memory present
blades hug the ether that surrounds me
ferrying whispers to and fro
while I listen to the inaudible
I am comforted by my unhearing
content in experience
I would live in my history
and its dead, but not for the promise
of life in a belly
a womb once within mine
gifting smiles, sword and shield,
there is no living without affliction
but the trembling cry of life
rallies legions from spent souls,
it promises
and threads my own skies
with histories of tomorrow.

Specifications

My body unblessed by the Rabbi
wasn't good enough
for your orthodox longings.

The bosom of your fantasy
spits forth a dance
like milk whisked in circles.

She doesn't exist
yet my head spins trying to keep her pace.
I'm haunted by the unliving thing in your head.

Tactic

When least expected
Reason embarks
as primordial emissary
straddling ventures,
girdling dreams,
and looming just long enough
to tease quandaries reaching
toward a loose thread
hanging from its coat tails.

The Catechist

We used to gorge on rainbows
I hate today
when I walk, I tread your flesh
The day was rare, a beauty
and it was vicious
It took you and my soul
The theft began with angels
singing sunlight,
with breezes soft and singular
heaven was near
but so was hell
and so hell made its mark
its stench right there
right on the breath of angels
hell hounds chomping at the bit
at your neck
and chaos whisking steel and brick
into your tomb, silent, still.
I remember your jacket
thank you for that
and I watch the movie, the pods
and remember your silly feet
you tried to kiss me,
then pretended to faint
who does that?
You were mine on my terms
and I couldn't appreciate the privilege
and I didn't follow the map
your cells mingle
with the new attraction
I tread your flesh
you hold thousands each day
on the cells of your back

these structures are your footprints
I walk in them
still unready and unholy.

The Giver

You never disappoint
Giving with one hand
Then scooping around
To grab back with the other
You always haul away more.
What a record -
Track marks cover my body
Like a collapsed labyrinth
Tracing paths from injection points
To emptied chambers.
When you hunger, you smile
Stretch out your hands
And I shrink away
But your reach is long,
You give again
Then drain me to ash.

The Herring Net

For every haul
a balance is necessary
A good day's catch
falls back into waves
without the boy balancing
on the boat's opposite side.

We play and win
expectant of repeat fortune
only to prevail bereft of coin
We can gorge on life
but without balance
we burst and die

Every addict begins with a taste
taste leads to pursuit
and obligation amnesia
We live the goldfish syndrome
chomp chomp chomp
bloat and die

Greed is the worm
it possesses Ouroboros
and he devours his tail
The cathartic power of complaint
soothes and fills
but chokes with a cure of dung.

For every haul
a balance is necessary
A good day's catch
falls back into waves
without alms to steady
a bounty on the counter side.

The Lovers

he gave silent council
with a smile or scowl
instruments apparent
to her alone
the unknown explanations
of their vague night opera
lie in shadow compelled
by an idle hand
that wanders, only slightly
only in utero
or more plainly
in vaults, motionless
appearing only as shapes
or shades of fabric
in their dance of unspoken love

The Night Cafe

Vincent's table
lays a game
that no one is playing
A man in white
the only one looking at me
more doctor than bus boy
Pool table, operating table
empty either way
My eyes draw to the open curtains
the light beyond is bright
and endless, perhaps entertaining
the occupant of an empty chair
Spirits crowd the buffet
set back and adorned with blooms
it seems an altar
Is it help? A cry in code
Father, doctor
in your white coat
the table's shadow
casts large enough to swallow it
like a coffin into a grave
In the café
goers chat drink and dine
deaf to the cry
blind to the orange and green
that play below the lights
a beautiful scream
desperate and unheard.

The Tragedy of Anne

Anne was Henry's best wife
the one he loved
forget the saintly
or the son bearer
Anne ruled his heart
for a time, she ruled
that fickle and feral heart
in those years
it danced in time to her music
and lulled to her poetry
through those years
he changed history
to possess this woman
an ordinary woman
who would change his nation
and slap the world into motion
unintentionally
the daughter who found love in duty
love beyond reach
for a time
she felt only sun from his eyes
and he saw only her
but the world is cruel
and the fates don't let us play
for free or for long
perhaps he hated her in the end
her end, a metaphor for reckless hearts
but look at the facts
no king has ever gone so far
no war waged since Troy
for love
no matter captivated that king
like hers

how Henry must have died
that day in May
and each day forward
history has written that
Anne lost her head
but with Anne,
that king lost his heart.

The Year of the Dragonfly

2020 what have you taught me so far?
So far I have learned that John wasn't high
he knew exactly what he was saying
about pestilence and war and death
you taught me that life is a thing
lethal with spines
it comes laden with catches
and trap doors, not rainbows
2020 you have taught me all about
the elusive, the stuff we take for granted
has teeth and jeers because we move too slowly
it's gone before we say the words
what have I learned 2020?
What color am I and why does it matter?
You have taught me to color outside the lines
because, 2020, we looked in the mirror
and know now that we don't blend
that was all a lie, an etiquette, a platitude
people are hurting in 2020
and you are making us die
2020 I have learned to say the words
quickly, before my breath is gone
before the ones I love are dead
before those who I love are angered
at my ignorance, and before I throw myself
weak and vulnerable toward a merciless world
filled with spines and violence
2020 I bleed at your spur
it hurts because my words come too late
but 2020 you brought me the dragonfly
he looked me in the eye
and now he is long gone
but I know what to say, I know it's late

and it's late again, but 2020 you taught me
that I can't, I won't catch up
so I say I love you
I love you I have to say it over and over
I'm too late. I say it
I love you. We say it too late
I love you I love you I love you.

Things I Miss

I miss the baseball
the running, the cold
and the heat
I miss being tired, broke
hungry and anxious
I miss his skinny arms
runny nose and big heart
and impatience
I miss toy trains and silly drawings

I miss dead people
their stories, their laughter
I miss how simple it was
to be happy
I miss the living, in our history
gathering at the stoop, here or there
or walking for walking's sake
taking turns to carry a boombox
telling tales, youth on parade

I miss breathing
the sound of my voice sickens me
as I whine of broken hearts
each word wasting joy
like pillows, smothering
swollen with feathers of regret
why do we plea probabilities?
why do we drown ourselves
in what we did's and what if's?

Unbuttoned

Looking for you
refuge in a soft blanket
but only if it is free,
you have a ring of many keys
but none unlock
so my heart is forked
by who you are
and who I need,
I knew it couldn't be
but didn't realize that
I didn't want it to be
My freedom meant more
it was that and not you
that seduced me
stirring in me
all that I am
Sadly, for me, it is that
which remains unattainable.

Validating Pluto

Hail Caesar
then strike him down
another clown
watch the senate play with themselves
they don't know
I'm bursting for relief
My daughter will be 19
and I'm not celebrating
you don't need to know her name
she doesn't need
cards, balloons, cake, pinata
as a matter of fact
let's just use pronouns…
health insurance won't stretch
unless she's a student
she can't do that, so she works
but her plan doesn't include the meds
or the care that she needs
which costs more than I make,
are you following?
she can't be a student
she needs an exam
she can't take it
until they call her
who are "they"?
your guess is as good as mine,
so she works for benefits
that don't include
mental health, of all things
but don't I live in a big city?
oh, forgive my rant.
I turn on the news
the senate is still playing with themselves

they want to break down the door
but Nero hasn't finished fiddling
my head is bursting
I go through my mail
she's not eligible for aid
because she works
she can't get a better job
because she needs a GED
and they have her on a waiting list
my head is bursting
I turn off the tv
and I remember that Pluto was a planet
until its benefits were yanked away
it's not a planet
it's not a rock
it's still there
like my nineteen year old
but it doesn't count, either
who decides that?
my head is bursting
but I've done some reading
in some countries
those who can't provide for their offspring
toss them from a mountaintop
before they grow or kill
before they wander onto subway platforms
and jump, or push grandmothers to the tracks,
they prevent the whole world
from flinching, saying, "uhhhhh!"
and wondering how it happened
are we better?
I read too much
my head will burst with relief
when the senate finishes playing with itself
so this is the edge of precipice

one foot on solid ground
waiting for a verdict
on Pluto, on a girl
with big brown eyes
that should count for something
like the last hundred years
as hulking, sulking wingman
of a solar system
now you see them
and now you still see them
but they don't count
my head is bursting
but the senate will never finish playing
Caesar is a clown
and Nero keeps on fiddling
at least the Romans did something
this senate is impotent
no good thing can come from it.

Well-known Unidentified

Mirroring the sky or ocean
or my mood sometimes
your range envelops the earth
every day painted in a hue
Known to all but the blind
yet even sightless, your depth
can be felt and feared
like endless night

names are on things that they love (I do have a few in my closet, but only if I like them). I hope that *they* buy, if they choose to, what *they* want. I hope that they don't feel forced to settle for less in anything, handbags, clothes, jobs or relationships. Above all, I hope that their relationships are without burden, and that the men in their lives are nurturing and generous.

"Kate, if you choose to marry, marry a wonderful man."